The Transcontinental Railroad

JOHN PERRITANO

Children's Press®
An Imprint of Scholastic Inc.
New York   Toronto   London   Auckland   Sydney
Mexico City   New Delhi   Hong Kong
Danbury, Connecticut

Content Consultant
David R. Smith, Ph.D.
Adjunct Assistant Professor of History
University of Michigan
Ann Arbor, Michigan

Library of Congress Cataloging-in-Publication Data

Perritano, John.
  The transcontinental railroad / by John Perritano.
      p. cm.—(A true book)
  Includes bibliographical references and index.
  ISBN-13: 978-0-531-20585-3 (lib. bdg.)   978-0-531-21248-6 (pbk.)
  ISBN-10: 0-531-20585-1 (lib. bdg.)   0-531-21248-3 (pbk.)

  1. Pacific railroads—Juvenile literature. I. Title. II. Series.

  TF25.P23P47 2010
  385.0973'0903—dc22   2009014185

All rights reserved. Published in 2010 by Children's Press, an imprint of Scholastic Inc.
Published simultaneously in Canada. Printed in China.
SCHOLASTIC, CHILDREN'S PRESS, A TRUE BOOK, and associated logos are trademarks and/or registered trademarks of Scholastic Inc.

1 2 3 4 5 6 7 8 9 10 R 19 18 17 16 15 14 13 12 11 10   62

Find the Truth!

Everything you are about to read is true *except* for one of the sentences on this page.

Which one is **TRUE**?

T or F The transcontinental railroad crossed Native American lands.

T or F Immigrants did not help build the transcontinental railroad.

Find the answers in this book.

3

Contents

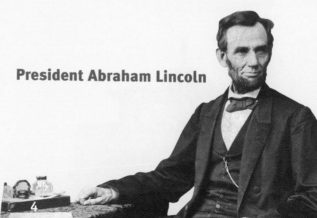

President Abraham Lincoln

4

Workers laid more than 1,700 miles of track for the transcontinental railroad.

THE BIG TRUTH!

Railroad Towns

5 End of the Line

10 MILES OF TRACK, LAID IN ONE DAY. APRIL 28TH 1869

In the 1830s, a barge was one kind
of boat that people could take
along the Erie Canal in New York.

6

CHAPTER 1

Rise of the Rails

In the early 1800s, the only way that people could travel throughout the United States was on foot or by boat or horse. In 1804, a British inventor built the first steam-powered **locomotive**. Soon after, the railroad came to the United States. By the end of the 1800s, people could travel from New York to California, or across the **continent**, by train. This transcontinental railroad would make travel faster and make many new things possible.

 Horses pulled barges along a path beside the Erie Canal.

Horse Against Train

The *Tom Thumb* was the first steam locomotive built in America. In 1830, there was a race between the *Tom Thumb* and a horse named Lightning. Each pulled a wagon full of people. The *Tom Thumb* was ahead until there was a problem with some of its machinery. In the end, Lightning won, but the *Tom Thumb* still proved that trains would be very useful in the future.

People joked that the *Tom Thumb* looked like a "teakettle on a track."

By 1835, there were more than 1,000 miles (1,609 km) of railroad track in the United States.

The Iron Horse

Most of the railroads were in the eastern part of the United States in the 1800s. Because moving supplies and people was easy by train, railroad companies began laying more track and building more trains. The Iron Horse, as people nicknamed the train, was here to stay.

Some gold seekers used pans to separate gold from dirt and other materials in the ground and water.

CHAPTER 2

Finding a Way West

In 1848, gold was discovered in California. As this news spread to the eastern part of the United States, people began moving west. At the time, there were only two ways for people to reach California. Both were long and difficult. They could take a train to Omaha, Nebraska. Then they would have to cross the Rocky Mountains on foot or by stagecoach, wagon, or horse. Travelers could also reach California by sailing around South America.

The value of all the gold mined during the California gold rush was $13 billion (in today's money).

A Solution

In 1850, about 55,000 **settlers** risked their lives traveling to California by wagon, hoping to strike it rich. In June 1859, thousands more made their way to Virginia City, Nevada, after gold and silver were discovered there. As people moved westward, a better and faster way to travel was needed more than ever. Many believed a railroad was the solution.

Between 1840 and 1860, about 300,000 people moved to the American West.

Finding a Route

In 1853, the U.S. Congress began looking for the best route for a railroad across America. **Surveyors** found five possible paths. A man named Theodore Judah tried to find a way for the railroad to pass through the Sierra Nevada of California. This mountain range was the largest obstacle a transcontinental railroad would face. In 1859, Judah went to Washington, D.C., to ask the U.S. Congress and President James Buchanan to support his plan.

Theodore Judah

The Issue of Slavery

Lawmakers in Washington liked the idea of a transcontinental railroad. But disagreements over slavery delayed construction for nearly 10 years. Many Southerners wanted the railroad to have a southern route so slavery could be spread to new **territories** in the West. Northerners believed a northern route could stop slavery from spreading. People in both areas knew businesses could make a lot of money by shipping their products to the West.

Dodge Finds a Way

As lawmakers argued, surveyors continued heading west to find a route. Surveyor Grenville Dodge found what he believed to be the easiest route. It followed the Platte River valley in Nebraska. Dodge had already looked at the route for another railroad company, so he knew of its possible problems. Eventually, this was the route chosen for the transcontinental railroad.

The Platte River and its branches extend across Nebraska and into Wyoming and Colorado.

The Platte River

A Divided Country

In 1861, Abraham Lincoln became president. Lincoln supported the idea of a transcontinental railroad. He thought it would bring the country together while helping America grow. But he did not want slavery to spread to western states and territories.

Several southern states that disagreed with the president over slavery **seceded** (suh-SEED-id), or left the United States. They formed their own country—the Confederate States of America. Soon after, the Civil War began.

Abraham Lincoln once worked as a lawyer for railroad companies.

Full Steam Ahead

The war did not stop plans for the transcontinental railroad. On July 1, 1862, just over a year after the war began, President Lincoln signed the Pacific Railroad Act. Under this law, the government would help two companies build a railroad across the continent. The Central Pacific Railroad would build east from Sacramento, California. The Union Pacific Railroad would lay track west from Omaha, Nebraska. They would eventually meet in Utah.

The red line on this map of the United States today shows the route of the Central Pacific Railroad. The blue line shows the route of the Union Pacific Railroad.

Civil War troops are transported
to the battlefield by train.

CHAPTER 3

America Gets on Track

The Civil War divided the nation, but the transcontinental railroad would unite the country. During the Civil War, there were more than 30,000 mi. (48,000 km) of railroad track in the United States. Trains were the fastest way to move armies and supplies. Sometimes army commanders used locomotives to send battle plans to their armies on the battlefield. All of this helped people understand how important trains could be to the country.

Many of the men who built the railroad had been soldiers in the Civil War.

Rails Across the Country

The government gave the railroad companies money and land for construction. The more track the companies put down, the more money they would make. In all, the Union Pacific laid about 1,000 mi. (1,609 km) of track. The Central Pacific, which had to cross the Sierra Nevada mountains in California, laid about 700 mi. (1,127 km) of track.

Construction on the railroad began on January 8, 1863.

Central Pacific workers lay down track for the transcontinental railroad.

The Big Four

The businessmen who ran the Central Pacific Railroad were called the Big Four. They were Leland Stanford, Charles Crocker, Collis P. Huntington, and Mark Hopkins. From the money raised to pay for the railroad to the actual construction, the Big Four oversaw every detail. A businessman named Thomas Durant also helped build the railroad. He was vice president of the Union Pacific Railroad.

The Central Pacific Railroad's first locomotive was named the Governor Stanford.

Leland Stanford was president of the Central Pacific Railroad from 1863 to 1893.

Taking Land

Several Native American tribes lived along the railroad's route. The U.S. government passed a law to help the railroad companies take over Native American land. The tribes, including the Sioux (SOO), Cheyenne (SHY-enn), Pawnee (PAW-nee), and Arapaho (uh-RA-puh-hoe), knew that the railroad would cause them many problems. Worse, settlers and railroad workers killed bison to make way for the farms and ranches that followed the railroad westward. Bison were important to Native Americans for food and clothing.

Fighting to Stop the Railroad

In response, Native Americans fought to protect their land. They attacked construction crews and ripped up track. The U.S. government decided to send in the army. Led by Civil War general William T. Sherman, troops destroyed many Indian villages. The fighting went on for years. Eventually, the Native peoples realized they could not stop the railroad from expanding across the United States.

Cheyenne Indians attack Union Pacific Railroad workers in Kansas in an attempt to keep the railroad from being built.

A Better Life

While construction of the railroad was not good for Native Americans living along its route, it helped other people by providing jobs. Most Union Pacific workers were Irish **immigrants**. Others were former slaves. Some workers had served as Confederate soldiers. Working on the railroad gave them steady paychecks. Although the pay was low, it was the most money these men had ever made.

Most railroad workers were paid about $35 a month.

Chinese Workers

The Central Pacific Railroad hired thousands of Chinese men. The company paid for the men's journey by ship from China to the United States. As railroad workers, they earned $1 a day. It was fair pay at the time. The Chinese—like all the railroad workers—spent long hours digging trenches and carving tunnels by hand. They even worked at night by firelight. By 1868, about 12,000 Chinese men were working on the railroad.

The Central Pacific Railroad began hiring Chinese workers in 1865.

A Union Pacific Railroad crew works on a rough section of ground.

CHAPTER 4

Working on the Railroad

Crews worked on the railroad in groups. Each group had a specific job. First, surveyors mapped out the route. **Graders** then cleared rocks and trees from the path and leveled the path through hills and over gaps. Another crew laid the rails. Right behind the rail layers came workers who hammered the spikes and rails into place. Finally, another group called track liners made sure the track was straight.

Union Pacific workers laid between 1 and 2 mi. (1.6 and 3.2 km) of track each day.

Workers use picks and sledgehammers to dig a tunnel.

Tools for a Tough Job

To get all of this work done, crews had only shovels, sledgehammers, wheelbarrows, picks, plows, and their bare hands. Teams of oxen pulled a board across the ground to smooth it out. Horses pulled wagons loaded with iron rails.

Each iron rail weighed 560 pounds (254 kilograms). Under the rails were wooden **ties**. Workers drove thick iron spikes into place to connect the rails to the ties.

Sherman Summit

The transcontinental railroad's builders faced many obstacles along the route. They had to blast through rock and cut down trees. One of the most difficult jobs was conquering Sherman Summit in Wyoming. The summit, between the towns of Laramie and Cheyenne, was the highest point on the line. Workers had to fill **gorges**, build bridges, and dig out tons of dirt before they could lay the track.

Workers cleared large rocks to build the Summit Tunnel.

Named for General William T. Sherman, Sherman Summit was 8,242 feet (2,512 meters) high.

Tunneling Through the Mountains

Central Pacific workers had to dig 15 tunnels through the mountains. To do this, they dug small holes in the rock. Workers filled the holes with blasting powder or dynamite and then lit a fuse. The explosion blew the rocks to bits, which were then removed. Before workers started using dynamite, they carved out only 8 inches (20 centimeters) of rock a day. Many workers died blasting through the mountains.

The Summit Tunnel

The Summit Tunnel

The Central Pacific Railroad workers had the toughest job of all. They had to cut through the **granite** of California's Sierra Nevada mountain range, which they reached in 1866. Winter blizzards and working along the edges of steep cliffs made construction even harder. Workers dug the Summit Tunnel through a peak that was 7,017 ft. (2,139 m) high. They worked 24 hours a day for a year to finish the 1,659-foot-long (506 m) tunnel.

Railroad Towns

As the Union Pacific and Central Pacific railroads laid down track, new towns sprang up along the route. Surveyors looked closely at the land that the railroads passed through. They divided that land into small pieces, which were sold to settlers. Settlers built the towns and cities that exist today.

Cheyenne

On July 4, 1867, workers pitched the first tents on the site that would become Cheyenne, Wyoming. Cheyenne grew into one of the largest towns along the railroad route.

Medicine Bow

The trains needed water to run. In 1868, the Union Pacific constructed a water-pumping station on the Medicine Bow River in Wyoming. Within a year, workers had built a small village and named it Medicine Bow.

Mormon workers cut a tunnel through the rock at Utah's dangerous Weber River Canyon.

CHAPTER 5

End of the Line

In the spring of 1868, railroad workers got some extra help. Swarms of grasshoppers had destroyed the crops of Utah farmers that year. Most of those farmers were members of the Mormon Church. With no other source of income, thousands of Mormons went to work for the Union Pacific. However, most workers never received the money owed to them. The company's Thomas Durant kept the money for himself and the railroad's **stockholders**.

Mormon workers prayed and sang at the end of the workday.

Crossing the West

Early in 1869, the Union Pacific workers made it through Wyoming and into Utah. However, work on the Central Pacific line went slower until the Summit Tunnel was finished. After that, Central Pacific workers were able to pick up the pace and quickly laid rail across Nevada and into Utah. As the end of construction neared, workers were in such a rush that they left many parts of the railroad unfinished or poorly built.

A Central Pacific crew at work in the mountains

Fast workers could put four 28-ft. (9 m) rails in place every four minutes.

Bad Behavior

The building of the transcontinental railroad was a huge project that involved many people both on and off the tracks. Behind the scenes, lawmakers and railroad officials got richer by the day as they stole money. This caused problems for workers because the stolen money was not being spent to buy the proper tools needed to build a safe railroad.

Without proper tools, many bridges along the railroad's route were not built to be safe enough for travel.

Race to the Finish

On April 9, 1869, the Union Pacific and the Central Pacific agreed that the two railroads would meet at Promontory Summit, Utah. Both companies raced to finish their sections of track. The Central Pacific men worked so fast that they completed the last 10 miles (16 km) of track in one day! Finally, on May 10, 1869, the two companies' locomotives—the Central Pacific's *Jupiter* and the Union Pacific's *Number 119*—had their historic meeting.

The railroad was completed seven years ahead of schedule!

10 MILES OF TRACK, LAID IN ONE DAY. APRIL 28TH 1869

This famous photograph shows the meeting of the locomotives at Promontory Summit on May 10, 1869.

"Wedding of the Rails"

With the end of construction, railroad officials hammered a golden spike into the track to cheers and applause from the many people who attended the celebration. A **telegraph** announced the end of the project to the nation, and with that the news quickly spread across the country. The message simply said, "Done!" Newspapers called the event a "wedding of the rails." The railroad had successfully united the nation.

Across the Continent

The completion of the transcontinental railroad affected almost all parts of American life. People could now travel from New York City to San Francisco, California, in seven days. While they were in the West, many people took advantage of an 1862 law that gave land to those willing to settle there. Soon millions boarded the trains and started new lives. The United States was growing as western territories, such as Utah and Montana, became states.

Timeline of the Transcontinental Railroad

July 1,
1862

President Abraham Lincoln signs the Pacific Railroad Act.

January 8,
1863

The Central Pacific Railroad begins construction in Sacramento, California.

Home Shopping

The transcontinental railroad helped businesses grow, too. Now companies could send goods such as bathtubs, sewing machines, and other products to settlers in the West. During each of the railroad's first 10 years, trains shipped $50 million worth of goods from coast to coast. Mail could also be carried from one side of the continent to the other.

Settlers in the West could order everything they needed for their homes and farms from the Sears, Roebuck and Co. catalog.

January 22, 1869

The Union Pacific lays its 1,000th mile of track.

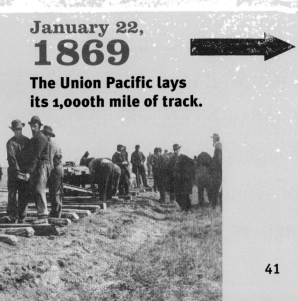

May 10, 1869

Railroad officials hammer the last spike into the rails at Promontory Summit, Utah.

Today, this former railroad tunnel is used by bicyclists and hikers.

Hundreds of miles of the original transcontinental rail line still exist.

Part of American Life

Each year, millions of people still travel the country by train. Railroads continue to transport goods such as coal, grain, and automobiles across the nation. Along the routes that are no longer used, tracks have been removed to make way for hiking and biking trails. Today, hikers and bikers can still enjoy the same sights that travelers saw from the windows of transcontinental railroad trains about 125 years ago. ★

True Statistics

Number of men who worked on the railroad from 1863 to 1869: 20,000

Total length of the railroad: 1,776 mi. (2,858 km)

Price of a first-class train ticket from New York to San Francisco in 1870: $136, or $2,288 in today's money

Most track laid in one day: 10 mi. (16 km) along the Central Pacific line on April 28, 1869

Length of a workday: Either 8 or 12 hours

Daily salary of Chinese workers: $1

Monthly salary of Irish workers: $35, plus living quarters

Typical meal the workers ate: Beef, pork, potatoes, onions, crackers, and coffee

A Central Pacific Railroad train schedule

Did you find the truth?

T The transcontinental railroad crossed Native American lands.

F Immigrants did not help build the transcontinental railroad.

43

Resources

Books

Blashfield, Jean F. *The Transcontinental Railroad.* Mankato, MN: Compass Point Books, 2002.

Blumberg, Rhoda. *Full Steam Ahead: The Race to Build a Transcontinental Railroad.* Washington, DC: National Geographic Society, 1996.

Evans, Clark J. *The Central Pacific Railroad.* New York: Children's Press, 2003.

Fine, Jill. *The Transcontinental Railroad: Tracks Across America.* New York: Children's Press, 2005.

Fraser, Mary Ann. *Ten Mile Day: And the Building of the Transcontinental Railroad.* New York: Henry Holt, 1993.

Houghton, Gillian. *The Transcontinental Railroad: A Primary Source History of America's First Coast-to-Coast Railroad.* New York: Rosen Central Primary Source, 2003.

Landau, Elaine. *The Transcontinental Railroad.* New York: Franklin Watts, 2005.

Olson, Nathan. *The Building of the Transcontinental Railroad.* Mankato, MN: Capstone Books, 2007.

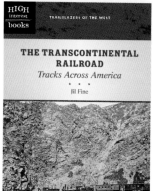

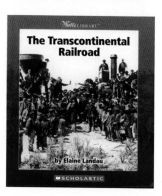

Organizations and Web Sites

American Memory: Railroad Maps
http://memory.loc.gov/ammem/gmdhtml/rrhtml/rrhome.html
Hundreds of railroad maps dating from 1828 to 1900 are located at this Library of Congress site.

Central Pacific Railroad Photographic History Museum
www.cprr.org/museum
View a collection of photographs that traces the history of the transcontinental railroad.

PBS American Experience: Transcontinental Railroad
www.pbs.org/wgbh/amex/tcrr
Find detailed information on the railroad, including maps and photos, and take a virtual road trip along the route.

Places to Visit

Golden Spike National Historic Site
P.O. Box 897
Brigham City, Utah 84302
(435) 471-2209, ext. 29
www.nps.gov/gosp
This site celebrates the completion of the first railroad to span the nation. Visitors can even drive along the original track route.

The Union Pacific Railroad Museum
200 Pearl Street
Council Bluffs, Iowa 51503
(712) 329-8307
www.uprr.com/aboutup/history/museum
View railroad photographs, documents, and Grenville Dodge's surveying equipment.

Important Words

continent – one of the earth's seven major areas of land. The continents are Africa, Antarctica, Asia, Australia, Europe, North America, and South America.

gorges – narrow spaces between rocky cliffs

graders – workers who level out roadways or other surfaces

granite – a hard stone that is created as a result of volcanic activity

immigrants – people who settle permanently in a country where they were not born

locomotive – an engine that pulls or pushes railroad cars. It can be powered by steam, electricity, or diesel fuel.

seceded (suh-SEED-id) – withdrew from a group

settlers – people who make their homes in a new area

stockholders – people with a financial interest in a company

surveyors – people who determine the boundaries of a route by measuring angles and distances with special instruments

telegraph – an instrument that uses electrical signals, in the form of coded signals, to quickly communicate over large distances

territories – regions that belong to and are run by a country

ties – pieces of wood that support the rails

Index

Page numbers in **bold** indicate illustrations

About the Author

John Perritano is an award-winning journalist and author of many nonfiction titles for children, including books on American history. He holds a master's degree in U.S. history from Western Connecticut State University. He is a former senior editor at Scholastic. He lives in Southbury, Connecticut, with his three dogs, three cats, and three frogs. He played with model trains as a child, and real trains fascinate him. He has written other True Books, including *The Lewis and Clark Expedition* and *Spanish Missions*.

PHOTOGRAPHS © 2010: Alamy Images: 3 (Lee Foster), 6, 10, 18 (North Wind Picture Archives), cover (The Print Collector); Bridgeman Art Library International Ltd., London/New York/Private Collection: 23 (by Jacob Gogolin/Peter Newark American Pictures), 40 right (© Look and Learn), 5 top, 41 bottom right (Peter Newark American Pictures); Central Pacific Railroad Photographic History Museum/CPRR.org: 36 (© 2009); Corbis Images: 8, 41 top, 43 (Bettmann), 5 bottom, 38 (George H.H. Huey), 15 (David Muench), 42 (Scott Smith), 25 foreground; Denver Public Library, Western History/Genealogy Department: 22 (by John Carbutt, Z-3297), 33 foreground (by Arundel C. Hull, Z-5816), 24 (Union Pacific Railroad Co., X-21535); Getty Images: 12 (American Stock Archive), 13, 21 (MPI); iStockphoto: 25 background, 32 background, 33 background (Evgueni Groisman), 32 foreground (Duncan Walker), 17 (ziggymaj); Library of Congress/Alexander Garner: 4, 16; National Archives at College Park: 39 (Department of Agriculture/ARC 594940); New York Public Library, Astor, Lenox and Tilden Foundation: 31 (Robert N. Dennis Collection of Stereoscopic Views/Miriam & Ira D. Wallach Division of Arts, Prints & Photographs); North Wind Picture Archives: 14, 30; Courtesy of Santa Fe Railway: 37; Scholastic Library Publishing, Inc.: 44; Stanford University Libraries: 29 (Department of Special Collections/Alfred A. Hart Photograph Collection); The Granger Collection, New York: 40 left; Union Pacific Museum, Railroad Photo Collection: back cover, 9, 28, 34, 41 bottom left; University of Nevada, Reno: 20 (Special Collections Department and University Archives); Utah State Historical Society: 26 (used by permission/all rights reserved).